Teaching Reiki *Your* Way

A GUIDE FOR REIKI MASTERS

Adrian Campbell, PhD

Copyright©2025 by Adrian Campbell, PhD
Cover and internal design by Adrian Campbell, PhD

All rights reserved. No part of this book may be reproduced in any form or by any electronic or mechanical means including information storage and retrieval systems - except in the case of brief quotations embodied in critical articles or reviews - without permission in writing from Adrian Campbell, PhD.

Published by Adrian Campbell, PhD
www.EnergeticPsyche.com

Table of Contents

Introduction 1
   Connecting to The Teacher Within 3
      Connecting to Your Why 4
      Embracing Diversity 9
Cultivating Your Ideal Class 19
      Music or Sound 22
      Movement 24
      Meditation 26
      Ritual 28
      Teaching Tips & Tidbits 34
      Dealing with Challenging Situations 37
Getting Down to Business 47
      Setting Your Fees 48
      Finding Class Space 49
      Teaching Online 54
      Equipment Needed: In-Person Classes 58
      Equipment Needed: Online Classes 60
      Websites & Marketing 63
      Insurance 66
      Class Registration & Enrollment 67

Reiki Class Outlines ……………………………………..71
    Standard Reiki Class Outlines …………………72
    Standard Class Prep Email ………………...……..74
    Usui Reiki Level I Class Outline ………………77
    Usui Reiki Level II Class Outline ……………...80
    Usui Reiki Level I/II Class Outline ……………83
    Usui Reiki Level III/ART Class Outline ………88
    Usui Holy Fire Reiki Level III/ART & Reiki Master Class Outline ……………………………90
Alternative & Online Reiki Class Outlines …………...99
    Alternative Reiki Outlines ……………………100
    Community Healing Attunement ……………..101
    Teaching Reiki Across Multiple Weeks ……...103
    Online Reiki Class Outlines …………………..105
    Online Class Prep Email ……………………...107
    Usui Reiki Level I Online Class Outline ……..111
    Online – Usui Reiki Level II Class Outline ….113
    Usui Reiki Level I/II Online Class Outline …..116
Guided Meditations & Experiences …………………..123
    Body Scan ……………………………………..124
    Protective Light Meditation …………………..130
    Holy Love Experience – Winding River ……..136
    Holy Love Experience – Waterfall …………...138

"Teachers change the world, one heart at a time"

Introduction

This book was written to help others more easily share the love of Reiki with the world. I became a Reiki Master in 2014 and have been teaching Reiki and mentoring practitioners ever since.

One thing I have heard time and time again from other Reiki Masters, is that they don't feel like they have enough support or experience to get started teaching their own classes.

As someone who has been teaching in multiple fields for over 20 years, teaching Reiki always came naturally to me, and honestly, it has been one of the greatest gifts of my life. I wanted to be able to share this gift with more than the Reiki Masters I worked with one-on-one, and so the idea for this book was born.

I hope you find the exercises and information provided to be helpful. I encourage you to remember that the students that are meant for you will find you, and the best way to ensure that, is to build a class that is unapologetically and authentically YOU.

Sending you so much Love & Light,

© 2025, Adrian Campbell, PhD

Connecting to the Teacher Within

Connecting to Your Why

Becoming a Reiki Master doesn't always automatically mean one will begin teaching. But for those who do connecting to your "Why" can be a very powerful tool, contributing to the design of your ideal class, helping to define how and where you want to teach, as well as who your ideal students might be.

Take a few moments in the space below to connect with your "Why". Why did you decide to teach Reiki? Do you have any hopes or expectations?

....

....

....

....

....

....

....

....

....

Now that you have spent some time connecting to your why, how do you think this will show up in the way you choose to teach your classes? What about the way you teach might be influenced by your particular why?

Teaching isn't always easy, but that isn't why we do it. One of the best ways to get you through some of those rough times is to connect back to your why.

Take a moment and jot down a few easy phrases that could help you connect to your why during a challenging moment.

....
....
....
....
....
....
....
....
....
....
....
....
....
....

Embracing Diversity

Diversity is what makes Reiki classes so awesome! Every single Reiki teacher is a unique and wonderful expression of Love. Even when we follow a specific curriculum, we still bring our own special spirit it to it.

Let's explore what makes you unique! Take a few moments to use the provided space to jot down (or draw) what you think makes up the essence of WHO you are.

Now, let's take a look at what came together to create your unique soul...

Take a few moments and fill in the circles across the next few pages with what makes you unique

Certifications & Education

Passions & Hobbies

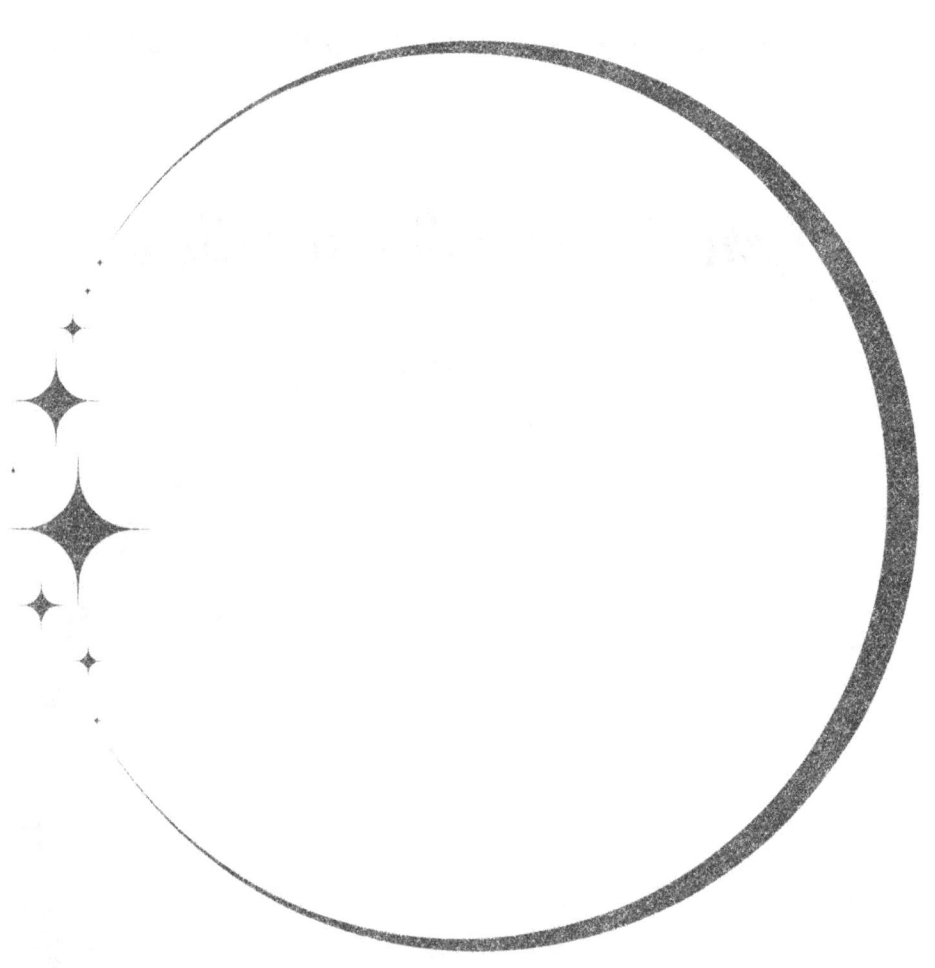

Your Spiritual Beliefs & Practices

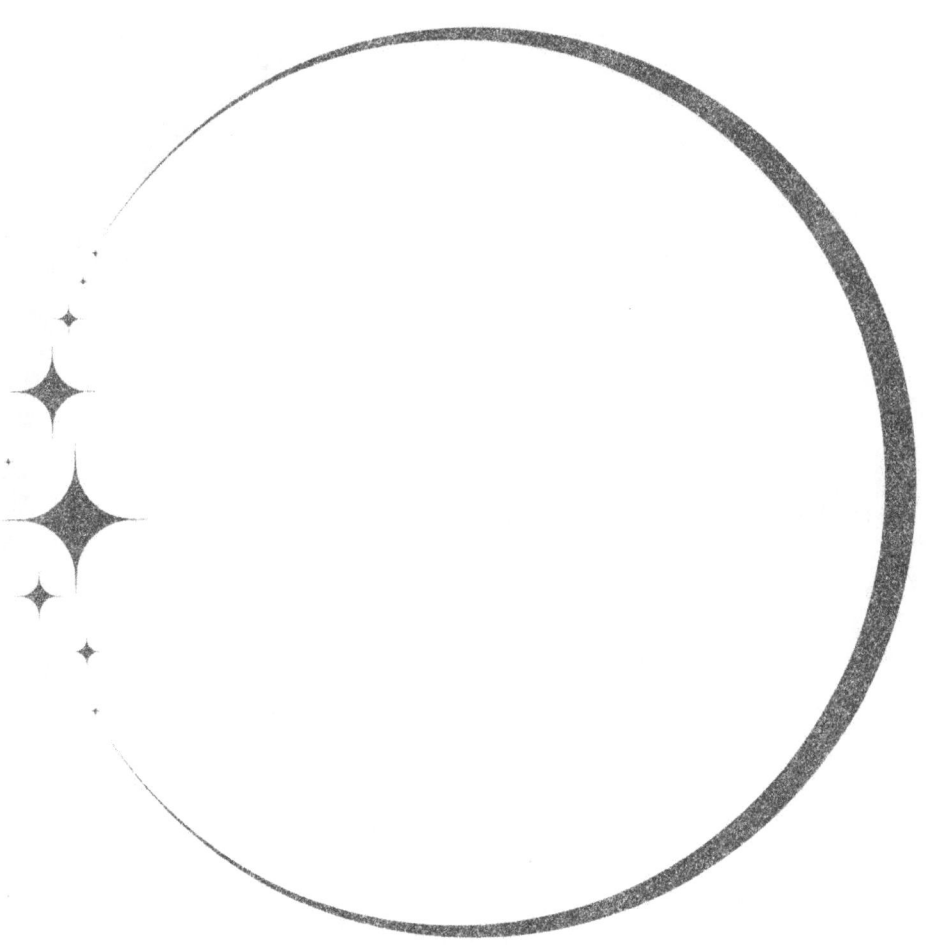

Your Wellness Practices

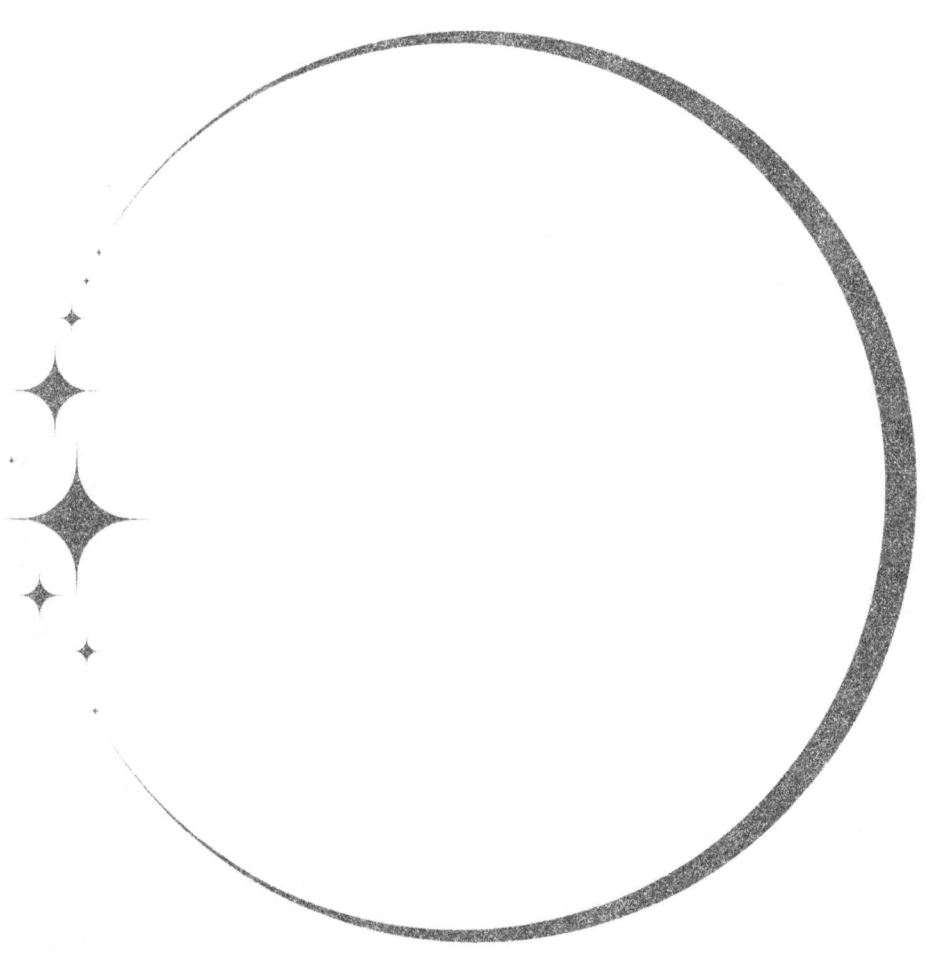

Reflecting on all that makes up the unique gift of YOU, what would you like to take into the classroom vs. what is important to keep as a practice just for you?

Cultivating Your Ideal Class

Cultivating Your Ideal Class

All the basics to teaching a Reiki class are included in the curriculum layouts at the end of this book, and if you do nothing more than follow along with those, you will teach a great class full of newly empowered Reiki Practitioners! But, why not add a little bit of what makes you special? After all, they were brought to your class for a reason.

The following pages will walk you through a few ideas for things you can add to your classes to make them more uniquely you. Explore the different areas, do some journaling, maybe some doodling, and feel free to let this stuff flex and flow as you develop your teaching style over time.

Music or Sound

Music or sound – singing bowls, chimes, chanting, meditative music, or you can even create a custom playlist with fun songs like Spirit in the Sky, or Don't Stop Believing. It really is up to you, just remember the sounds we use should fit who we are and the environment we are trying to create.

What Music might you want to use to play as students arrive?

During your meditations?

During attunements?

As a movement break?

As a closing to the day?

Movement

Movement … think yoga, somatic mindfulness, walking meditation, Reiki showers, aura cleanses, dancing, or just open space to let them move however they want.

What type of movement might you want to add to your class?

Would it be towards the beginning, as a break to get energy flowing, or as part of your teaching?

Meditation

At the back of this book are a few meditations for you to choose from, but feel free to use any of your own that you feel comfortable with.

Some different options could include breathwork or a simple body scan to help ground and center, a guided meditation leading them to their heart space, or a guided meditation (with or without Reiki) leading them through their seven major chakras.

What type of meditation or guided experience might you consider adding to your Reiki classes?

Ritual

Ritual can be a very important piece of Reiki trainings, and varies widely from teacher to teacher. When choosing which ritual practices to share, it is a good idea to consider who your students typically are and which rituals would best support their Reiki experience.

Whatever you choose, be intentional and ensure that you choose something that has meaning for you.

Some simple ideas include building a community altar, lighting a candle at the beginning of each class, or clearing the room together using Reiki.

What rituals are important for you at the beginning of something new? What helps create a container for you?

Bringing it all together...

Take a few minutes to lay out what your ideal class might look like with all these different elements brought together.

Feel free to record your ideas as words or images, in black and white, or full color! Get creative and let your imagination take over.

Teaching Tidbits & Tips

- Your #1 job is to hold space – create a container that helps the students to feel safe and secure for what will take place, physically, psychologically, and spiritually.

- Be prepared to teach, and know that nothing is ever perfect, something will most likely go wonky, and that is OK. Rely on your training, not just the plan, and trust in the fact that you are never alone when teaching Reiki, Spirit is there to support you.

- No one knows you "messed up" until you tell them.

- Providing the opportunity to journal and share can be just as important as the meditative experience itself.

Be careful not to place a value on someone's share.

Instead of saying that someone's experience was good or bad, try statements like "How interesting" or "What a unique experience" or "Thank you for sharing".

 Things will shift and you may need to adjust your class schedule… choose what your priorities are, so if this happens you know what to "let go of" easily.

For example: If you are short on time, you can skip or skim through certain sections in the book because they can read that on their own later, but they won't always have the teacher around or be able to practice on another person.

Let them know they will have journaling time after the meditation/experience for 5-10min. You don't need to give them that amount of time exactly, but it helps them know they have time to more deeply explore what may have come up.

After about 5 minutes look to see where they are at, and if everyone is done early you can end the time early. If not, a tip for ending gently is to give a heads up a couple minutes before… "So we'll journal for just a couple more minutes…" and then when you are ready to end journaling "I invite you to find a comfortable place to stop and bring your attention back to the group".

Dealing with Challenging Situations

A Student's Beliefs are in Opposition to Your Own

This is almost guaranteed to happen at some point. What is important to remember is that unless your class is one that combines multiple modalities AND that was specifically identified in your class description, you are teaching Reiki, and that is it. Reiki isn't a religion and is practiced by many different people around the world of varying spiritual beliefs, including atheism. Your responsibility as a Reiki Master is to share the love of Reiki, not to define what it means to the individual receiving it.

You never know who will end up in your classroom, but you can always ask about their beliefs or experience working with energy as part of the introductions in class, or even on a phone call ahead of class.

Because so many people relate to Source in different ways, it can be helpful to be prepared to use more general terms when describing the source of Reiki energy, such as "Source", Spirit", or "Universe".

A Student is Crying

Crying before, during, or after reiki is common. It is a natural way for the body to release whatever needs to be expressed. For this reason, it is encouraged that you provide at least one box of tissues in your classroom. At the beginning of your class feel free to talk about this and share that if someone is crying it is an act of respect to allow them that process. When we reach out to "comfort" someone who is crying, either through an offer of tissues or a gentle touch, we are often trying to minimize our own discomfort, not theirs. Share with the students that their tears are sacred expressions and allowed to flow.

Let them know that they are encouraged to take care of themselves as they need to, including leaving the room for a moment, though they are encouraged to stay.

Every once in a while a student may have an intense emotional response to something in class which could cause sobbing or a more hysterical type of crying. If you notice that the student is having difficulty moving through the release (can't stop crying hysterically), put the class on a break and speak with the student individually. You are encouraged not to practice outside your level of expertise, if you aren't a therapist, don't try to act like one. You can however ask the student what they might need in the moment (space, a drink of water, a few breaths) and do what you can to help them find that. At the end of the day, they will know what is best for them, your job is to hold space for the class. When you return to the class, acknowledge that the student needed some time, but do not share about their private experience. You may need to do a centering exercise to bring the class back together, and then you can continue on.

A Student Leaves the Room Upset

If a student leaves the room upset, first, do not immediately assume it is something you did or said. During Reiki training lots of stuff comes up that may or may not have anything to do with what you are sharing at the time. Give the student the space they need by not immediately following them out, and if they aren't back within 15-20 minutes, put the class on break and go check on them.

One Student is Taking Up all the Class Time

Unfortunately, this happens more often than you might think. Usually, it is someone that is just really excited to be surrounded by people who they resonate with and they can't help but ask a lot of questions and share all about all of their experiences.

In the case of too many questions, you can ask for them to hold their questions or write them down until you are ready to answer them, which may be on break. If the questions are off topic, feel free to say that. An example of languaging could be "That is an interesting question, but a little off topic. Our time together is limited, so I am going to have to skip that so we can focus on Reiki for now". You can also be direct when you ask for anyone that would like to share to minimize detours, example of languaging could be "We have a just a few minutes to share, is there anyone who would like to give a few words that would sum up their experience?" or "If there was one word that could express the felt sense of your experience, what would it be?"

Every once in a great while, you may encounter a student who treats the Reiki class like their very own personal healing session or as if they are the teacher, both demonstrate very similar behaviors. This person will often monopolize the group share time, talk across the group answering and asking questions of others while you are teaching, and ask questions that are deeply personal in nature, both of others and about themselves. This can be difficult to deal with, but it is important that you do, so you will be able to honor and hold space for the entire class.

You can start with the methods listed above, and if those don't work, you may need to pull them aside for a chat on break. Examples of languaging you could use include, "I am really glad that you are so engaged and excited to learn, but there are multiple people in class and we only have so much time to share and ask questions. If you could try to write down your thoughts and only share a brief description, that would be so helpful."

Or "You obviously have a lot of experience and expertise in the area of (crystals), as much as I appreciate the information you are sharing, my class outline is pretty focused and I need to be sure we stay on track. Can you help me out by saving that information for during our breaks?"

If all else fails… Take a break and a couple breaths!

Remember, you got this and you are never alone when you are teaching Reiki. Every teacher that came before you and every teacher currently practicing is energetically connected to you. Reach out and feel the strength of that connection, and know that no matter what Spirit has your back. Be curious and compassionate and you'll do just fine.

Take a few minutes to think about a teacher you admire, how do you imagine they might handle some of the issues that come up in class?

Maybe you have been in a class where the teacher did a great job dealing with a difficult situation, what happened and what did they do?

Getting Down to Business

Setting Your Fees

Setting your fees for classes depends on many different factors, including your background and level of experience, the location of your classes, what will be included in the experience (materials, extra services, etc.), and the layout/timeline you decide to use to deliver the information.

A good way to create a baseline price is to do an internet search for teachers, wellness centers or other professional organizations in your area and set your prices in a way that aligns with theirs. If you plan to offer something additional in your classes, or bring something unique that people would normally pay extra for, don't be afraid to charge a little more.

Remember they aren't paying for your time, they are paying for the hours and hours of training and experience you have, and you deserve to be compensated for your efforts.

You deserve to charge what your peers are charging, and remember that when you charge too little, you not only hurt yourself by disrespecting the time and effort you put into your offerings, but you also undercut the Reiki community.

That being said, Reiki is about sharing love and if you feel guided to gift a few seats in your classes, or give discounts to specific students, there is nothing wrong with that. Find what works best for you, and if all else fails, reach out to a few other Reiki Masters and see what they recommend.

Finding Class Space

There are several different options for where to hold your class, it really comes down to the experience you want to provide.

Typical Reiki classes have anywhere from 3 to 15 students, so the space you choose should be able to accommodate the class size you are expecting, including chairs in a circle and tables for practice (1 table for every 3 students is ideal). Most Reiki Masters rent space for their classes from wellness centers, metaphysical stores, or yoga studios, which not only provides space but often marketing which is especially helpful if you are a newer teacher. Pricing can range from $100/day to $500+/day, depending on you location and the type of space you are renting. If you are trying to save a little money and don't need the marketing help those types of places will bring you, try exploring other wellness-oriented businesses that often close on the weekend and might have group space (e.g., therapist offices, chiropractors, or even local colleges).

Allow yourself to think outside the box, take your time and find the right space for you and your students.

Meditate with Reiki and ask for guidance, pay attention to synchronicities, and connect with your community for anything they might know of.

A few things to consider are:

 Who are you sharing the space/building with? As mentioned, being in a space with other wellness professionals can have major advantages when it comes to referrals, and they often have a higher level of understanding around the need to maintain a relaxing environment. If you choose to go a different route, be sure to be very clear about your need for privacy and quiet.

 Are you allowed to organize the room the way you want to? Will there be chairs available? Floor cushions, mats? What about a refrigerator, water cooler? Restrooms?

Pay attention to street noise and noise from any other business that is close. Check out the inside of your space during the time of day you plan to teach so you can get a good idea of the noise level. It is really challenging to provide a calm and relaxing environment when you share a wall with a busy restaurant.

 If there is no refrigerator, be sure you are close enough to restaurants that your students can grab something for lunch, or you will need to provide more time for them to do so.

 Ask what is expected of you as far as costs, clean-up, etc.

 If you are renting space, be sure to sign a contract that includes cancellation policy and fees, insurance requirements, date and times of your class.

 The pressure of needing to enroll a certain amount of students can negatively impact your class, so be realistic with your budget before you decide on a space.

If you only enroll 2-3 students will you be OK financially? Class size will always vary, remember we are brought who we are meant to work with.

If you are a newer teacher and don't have a large following, consider starting somewhere small or more informal and work your way up to a large space.

If you are working one-on-one with a student you can teach just about anywhere you would do your normal sessions, as long as you have space to sit together and chat. You will also need to make sure you have privacy, so even though teaching Reiki on the beach sounds awesome, you would want to ensure that you aren't being watched during the attunement process.

Teaching Online

Teaching Reiki online can be done both one-on-one or with a full class, but it is a very different experience for both the teacher and the students, not good or bad, just different. The primary difference being the lack of hands-on practice in class with other students, which may make online training less beneficial for students who would benefit from a higher level of support and guidance during practice. Dr. Campbell's online classes have a unique outline and are provided later in this book.

Though she teaches Levels I-III, and other Reiki oriented classes online, Dr. Campbell does not recommend teaching Reiki Master online.

Due to the container that is created, the Reiki Master level of training should be done in person if at all possible.

Things to consider when teaching online:

 Teach smaller classes, maximum of 8 is recommended, as it becomes more difficult to hold space with everyone in their own environments.

 Be sure to list technology requirements ahead of time, as your students need to use a computer, NOT a phone. When students use a phone, it can become distracting for the class and more technical issues are often encountered.

 Students should have their audio and video on at all times, just as they would in class together. Communities aren't silent, people cough, dogs bark, we're in it together.

- Choose a platform you are comfortable with (Dr. Campbell uses Zoom) and be sure to hold a few practice events on your own, or with a friend to work out as many bugs as you can in advance.

- Allow extra time at the beginning of class, as that is when most technical issues arise. You may want to consider planning something that students can "walk into" without disturbing the class for the first 30 minutes.

- ALWAYS have a back-up plan and share with the students in the beginning of class. What happens if they get "kicked off"?

What happens if YOU get kicked off? What will you do if you lose Wi-Fi? Can you use your phone as a hotspot? What if your computer dies? Are you comfortable enough to use your phone? Know the answers to these questions BEFORE your class.

Consider using the "Lock" feature (on Zoom) to secure the room during meditations and attunements to minimize interruptions, this ensures that if someone is bumped offline, they have to wait for your approval to come back in. Ensure that you communicate this with the class, so they know what to expect.

 Please do not feel like you have to go beyond your level of comfort with technology. Can you use breakout rooms, polls, and all the other features? Sure, but your students may not know how to, and that is one more layer of teaching you will need to do. The beauty of Reiki is its simplicity. Show up online and end on time, and you'll do great.

Equipment Needed: In-Person Class

The following items are recommended with notations on which are optional:

 Class manuals – 1 per student, plus 1 extra (always have an extra!)

Dr. Campbell's Reiki manuals for Levels I&II, and Level III ART/Master, are available online. Bulk order discounts are available by contacting her team online at www.EnergeticPsyche.com

 Portable speaker* to play music during meditations. It is highly recommended NOT to use your phone as a speaker.

 Quartz Crystal point in small drawstring bag – 1 per student

(optional, but highly recommended if using Dr. Campbell's manual)

- Reiki Tables* – 1 per every 3 students

  (12 students = 4 tables, 9 students = 3 tables, 7 students = 3 tables, 4 students = 2 tables).

  Simple massage tables can be found online ranging from $75-$300+. The less expensive tables are typically lighter and easier to move, just ensure the weight limit and width/length will be appropriate for most students.

- Flat sheet (twin size) or blanket - one per table

- Pillows (for head), blankets* (for comfort/pillow), bolsters* (for under knees) - all optional BUT highly recommended)

- Colored pencils - 1 set per student (optional)

- Printed and signed certificates – 1 per student and 1 blank just in case there is a spelling error.

- Journal - 1 per student (optional)

*note that if you rent space from a yoga studio or other wellness space, some of these items may be included in the rental rate, saving you from having to buy and transport them yourself.

Equipment Needed: Online Class

The following items are recommended with notations on which are optional:

- Class manuals*** – 1 per student. Dr. Campbell's Reiki manuals for Levels I&II, and Level III ART/Master, are available online. Bulk order discounts are available by contacting her team online at www.EnergeticPsyche.com

- Printed and signed certificates

    1 per student to be electronically delivered at the completion of the class.

- Computer and video camera

- Proper lighting – Ensure that you show up well on video and if necessary, consider a ring light.

- Zoom (or other platform) account – ensure it has multiple hour and attendee capability.

    Also, be sure to let your students know if they need to download or set anything up in advance to participate on your chosen platform.

- Quartz Crystal points in small drawstring bag*** – 1 per student. (optional, but highly recommended if using Dr. Campbell's manual)

***Options for items needed by online students:

1) Order the Reiki manuals online to be delivered directly to your students and ask each student to go crystal shopping for their own quartz point.

2) Mail each student a package containing a Reiki manual, a crystal in a bag, a journal, and maybe a nice note card. It takes a bit more effort, and costs a bit more, BUT it is such a lovely gesture and helps create connection, which is even more important when teaching online.

One possible issue you may encounter with this option is last minute registration. To avoid this being an issue either close registration two weeks prior to ensure you have enough time for shipping, or have a back-up plan (i.e., Ship the book straight from Amazon 2day delivery and tell them they have to go buy a quartz point).

Websites & Marketing

Depending on whether you plan to teach primarily online or in-person will make a world of difference when deciding how to market your classes. Some teachers go the route of the internet, working to create a large online presence and gather students for their classes that way. Others put their efforts into marketing to their local community, and many do both. Whatever you choose, just be sure that it is in alignment with who you are. Remember that every Reiki Master is unique, so are their offerings, and the way they move through the world. It is completely ok to do a bit of market research and apply techniques you see others using, but remember to honor who you are as a teacher and share your offerings in accordance with that.

Websites and online media management can be costly, whether you do it yourself or hire out, remember that even if you don't pay for it with cash money, you are still paying for it with your time.

Having an online presence is helpful, as most Reiki classes tend to be $200+ some people need time to make their decision, and the info you provide online can be a place they can visit on their own time to help become more informed and comfortable with the idea of becoming a Reiki practitioner.

As awesome as having an online presence is, creating community is what matters most (both online and in-person). If you want to market your business you have to meet people beyond more than a "like" and a "follow" online. I know many individuals in the wellness industry are more of the introverted type, and that is ok.

Some great ideas to get started include:

- Schedule time to have coffee/tea with wellness center owners (yoga studios, metaphysical stores, etc.)

It can be less intimidating than just walking in and trying to have a conversation in their place of business, plus it gives you an opportunity to get to know each other and who knows, maybe they have been waiting for someone just like you!

 Have a booth at wellness/holistic fair. You can offer to be a speaker and share about Reiki, market your classes, and/or offer 10 min chair sessions for $10ea.

 Look up other Reiki Masters and wellness practitioners in town and schedule time to chat, either in-person, on the phone, or a video chat. Ask about their offerings and business, who they work with and what their specialties are, and share the same about your business with them. Remember, there is no competition and having others to refer people to when something is outside of your scope is so helpful.

Remember that not everyone you meet is going to be a friend or interested in what you have to offer, and that is OK. Again, those meant for you will find you. Be gentle with yourself, only go where it feels right, and trust that things will align in the best interest of you and your students.

Insurance

Insurance is recommended if you are going to be working with others in a professional capacity. It isn't very expensive, around $100/year, and there are multiple options online for you to choose from. It provides peace of mind for you and shows those you choose to work with that you are serious about your business. In addition, many wellness centers, yoga studios, and holistic fairs require you to have insurance to rent space.

Class Registration & Enrollment

Class registration and enrollment can be as simple or as complicated as you want it to be. There are many wonderful CRM (Customer Relationship Management) platforms out there to help you manage your customer interactions, including registration for events. If your business isn't quite ready for a CRM, you can use an online event registration service, like Eventbrite, or even keep it old school, and just make a list.

One big benefit of the online programs is little to no interaction is required from you once you put in all the information and get it set up. However, they do have a fee, and many Reiki teachers like to have more control over who is joining their classes, which is difficult with an online auto-registration system. A nice in-between is to have an automated system (like Calendly) so interested students can schedule a call with you. From that point on you can enter them into your CRM or add them to your student list, it's up to you.

Reiki Class Outlines

Standard Reiki Class Outlines

The following class outlines are considered "standard" because they are currently the most commonly offered layouts for Reiki classes, but that doesn't mean they are the ONLY way to teach Reiki. They are provided as guidance to help create a strong foundation for you to grow from. Please note that the chapters and meditations listed in the class outlines are referencing Dr. Campbell's Reiki class manuals "Learn to Practice Reiki", "Become a Reiki Master", and this book, "Teach Reiki Your Way".

Each class includes the bare minimum required to be considered a "certificate course". As mentioned previously, many teachers opt to add in more material, just keep in mind if you delete any of the fundamentals you risk straying away from teaching a "Reiki" class. This is OK, Dr. Campbell herself has created multiple courses that include Reiki attunements but don't certify individuals to become practitioners.

Just be sure that you are clear about what you are providing your students, so they don't think they are getting certified as practitioners, if they aren't.

Also included are templates for prep emails to be sent out to your students at least one week in advance of the class, to help them prepare.

It is recommended that you use the provided outlines and email templates as a foundation to write-up your own outlines which will include the elements that truly make the class yours.

Please note that this book is designed to support trained Reiki Masters. For more information on Reiki Training please see Dr. Campbell's books, "Learn to Practice Reiki" and "Become a Reiki Master"

Standard Class Prep Email

Greetings,

I'm excited to share the magic of Reiki with you this Weekend! Below is some info to help you prepare for the class.

Note: I need you to email me back with the name you want on your certificate by (enter date here).

Class Date:
Location:
Time:

A few bits of guidance...

- Please bring a journal or notebook and something to write with. I invite you to bring a highlighter or tabs, as well as colored pencils/crayons/markers for any journaling we do after our meditations.

- Dress comfortably, and feel free to bring fluffy socks or a blanket.

Standard Class Prep Email (Cont.)

- You are invited to use meditation cushions, or things of that nature to sit on/with. (Let them know here if you will be sitting at desks/tables or if you will be sitting on the floor/in a chair). Please bring anything you would like to make your time more comfortable.

- There are no planned breaks, but I usually try to take one every hour or so, or as needed. And there will be a break for lunch, but no set time.

- Hot/cold filtered water is available, bring a water bottle if you'd like.

- Lunch will be 45-60ish minutes, feel free to bring your lunch to enjoy in the studio (no fridge FYI), and there are also quite a few places in town that you can grab something from if you'd prefer that.

Standard Class Prep Email (Cont.)

- To physically prepare: do your best to abstain from, or minimize alcohol, meat products, caffeine, and maintain a "clean" diet. Not a requirement, just do what feels right for your body. Please be sure to do your best to get a good night's sleep before class.

- To mentally prepare: try to spend some time in meditation every day, play attention to your dreams, and any other synchronicities that might occur.

If you have any other questions please let me know. My cell is (Phone number here) in case you need to text/call me. I am looking forward to our class together.

See you Saturday!

(Your Name here)

Usui Reiki Level I
Class Outline (8hrs)

- Logistics & Safety: Share start/end time of class, break policy, location of restrooms/exits/water. (5min)
- Review of materials needed for class: (5min)
    - Class manual: "Learn to Practice Reiki" (have them write their name inside)
    - Journal/something to write in & with
- Intros – Ask students to share their name, any experience with energy healing, and their expectations for the class (20-30min)
- Share your Reiki story with the students (5-10min)
- Holy Love Guided Experience - Winding River, journaling & share (15-30min)
- Chapter 1: Getting to know the Energetic Body (60min)

Usui Reiki Level I
Class Outline (8hrs) cont.

- Chapter 2: Understanding Reiki Energy (60min)
- Chapter 3: Energy Healing Techniques (60min)

Lunch (30-60min)

- Level 1 attunement, journaling, & share (30-60min)
- Practice flowing Reiki as a group with hands in prayer (Gassho) position (10-15min)
- Guide students through practice of a self-healing using standard hand placements, journaling, group share (30-45min)
- Hand out certificates
- Closing meditation of your choice.

Usui Reiki Level I
Class Outline (8hrs) cont.

Notes:

Times listed are approximate and will vary based on number of students and the questions asked. When you take lunch will vary on your start/end time but is suggested before or after Chapter 3 if possible.

The chapters and meditations listed are referencing information from Dr. Campbell's Reiki class manuals "Learn to Practice Reiki" and "Become a Reiki Master".

Usui Reiki Level II
Class Outline (8hrs)

- Logistics & Safety: Share start/end time of class, break policy, location of restrooms/exits/water. (5min)
- Review of materials needed for class: (5min)
    - Class manual: "Learn to Practice Reiki" (have them write their name inside)
    - Quartz Crystal in bag
    - Journal/something to write in & with
- Intros – Ask students to share their name, any experience with energy healing, and their expectations for the class (20-30min)
- Share your Reiki story with the students (5-10min)
- Holy Love Guided Experience - Waterfall, journaling & share (15-30min)
- Chapter 4: The Healing Power of Crystals (30-60min)

Usui Reiki Level II
Class Outline (cont.)

- Chapter 5: Using Reiki Energy with Others (30min)
- Chapter 6: Usui Holy Fire Reiki Level II Symbols (60min)

Lunch & Symbol Practice (60min)

- Level II Symbol "Test" (30min)
- Level II attunement, journaling, & share (30-60min)
- Practice giving Reiki in groups of 2-4. Start with Reiki & no symbols, and then add symbols to note the difference (60min)
- Guide students through a distance Reiki session (20min)
- Guide students through using Choku Rei to seal and clear the space (15min)
- Chapter 7: Working with Reiki in Everyday life (60min)

Usui Reiki Level II
Class Outline (cont.)

- Practice in groups of 2-4 using guide from Ch.7 on giving a "Complete Reiki Session" (60min)
- Chapter 8: Doing Business as a Reiki Practitioner (optional)
- Hand out Certificates
- Closing meditation of your choice

Notes:

Times listed are approximate and will vary based on number of students and the questions asked. When you take lunch will vary on your start/end time, but should occur before the attunement.

The chapters and meditations listed are referencing information from Dr. Campbell's Reiki class manuals "Learn to Practice Reiki" and "Become a Reiki Master".

Usui Reiki Level I/II Class Outline (2 Days)

Day one:

- Logistics & Safety: Share start/end time of class, break policy, location of restrooms/exits/water. (5min)
- Review of materials needed for class: (5min)
  - Class manual: "Learn to Practice Reiki" (have them write their name inside)
  - Quartz Crystal in bag
  - Journal/something to write in & with
- Intros – Ask students to share their name, any experience with energy healing, and their expectations for the class (20-30min)
- Share your Reiki story with the students (5-10min)
- Holy Love Guided Experience - Winding River, journaling & share (15-30min)
- Chapter 1: Getting to know the Energetic Body (60min)

Usui Reiki Level I/II Class Outline (cont.)

- Chapter 2: Understanding Reiki Energy (60min)
- Chapter 3: Energy Healing Techniques (60min)

Lunch (30-60min)

- Level 1 attunement, journaling, & share (30-60min)
- Practice flowing Reiki as a group with hands in prayer (Gassho) position (10-15min)
- Guide students through practice of a self-healing using standard hand placements, journaling, group share (30-45min)
- Provide students with a copy of the level II symbols, briefly explaining each one and that they will need to verbally name and draw each one by memory the following day.
- Closing meditation of your choice.

Usui Reiki Level I/II Class Outline (cont.)

Notes:

Times listed are approximate and will vary based on number of students and the questions asked. When you take lunch will vary on your start/end time but is suggested before or after Chapter 3 if possible.

The chapters and meditations listed are referencing information from Dr. Campbell's Reiki class manuals "Learn to Practice Reiki" and "Become a Reiki Master".

Usui Reiki Level I/II Class Outline (cont.)

Day Two

- Check-in with students - How is everyone feeling? Any questions come up overnight?
- Holy Love Guided Experience - Waterfall, journaling & share (15-30min)
- Chapter 4: The Healing Power of Crystals (30-60min)
- Chapter 5: Using Reiki Energy with Others (30min)
- Chapter 6: Usui Holy Fire Reiki Level II Symbols (60min)

Lunch & Symbol Practice (60min)

- Level II Symbol "Test" (30min)
- Level II attunement, journaling, & share (30-60min)
- Practice giving Reiki in groups of 2-4. Start with Reiki & no symbols, and then add symbols to note the difference (60min)

Usui Reiki Level I/II
Class Outline (cont.)

- Guide students through a distance Reiki session (20min)
- Guide students through using Choku Rei to seal and clear the space. (15min)
- Chapter 7: Working with Reiki in Everyday life (60min)
- Practice in groups of 2-4 using guide from Ch.7 on giving a "Complete Reiki Session" (60min)
- Chapter 8: Doing Business as a Reiki Practitioner (optional)
- Hand out Certificates
- Closing meditation of your choice

<u>Notes</u>:

Times listed are approximate and will vary based on number of students and the questions asked. When you take lunch will vary on your start/end time, but should occur before the attunement.

The chapters and meditations listed are referencing information from Dr. Campbell's Reiki class manuals "Learn to Practice Reiki" and "Become a Reiki Master".

Usui Reiki Level III/ART Class Outline (8hrs)

- Logistics & Safety: Share start/end time of class, break policy, location of restrooms/exits/water. (5min)
- Review of materials needed for class: (5min)
    - Reiki manual (have them write their name inside)
    - Quartz Crystal in bag
    - Journal/something to write in & with
- Intros – Ask students to share their name, what energy healing training they have, and their expectations for the class (20-30min)
- Share your Reiki story with the students (5-10min)
- Holy Love Guided Experience - Winding River, journaling & share (15-30min)
- Chapter 1: Setting a Foundation (30min)
- Chapter 2: Reiki Level III/Art (30min)
- Chapter 2: … The Healing Power of Crystals Crystals (30min)

Usui Reiki Level III/ART
Class Outline (cont.)

- Chapter 2: ... Exploring the Chakra System (30-60min)
- Chapter 2: ... Reiki Master Symbol (20min)

Lunch & Symbol Practice (60min)

- Dai Ko Myo Symbol "Test"
- Chapter 2: ... Understanding Attunements (30-60min)
- Attunement to Dai Ko Myo, journaling & share (30-60min)
- Demonstrate a Healing Attunement (10min)
- Practice in groups 2-3 giving each other Healing Attunements (30-60min)
- Hand out Certificates
- Closing meditation of your choice

Notes:

Times listed are approximate and will vary based on number of students and the questions asked.

The chapters and meditations listed are referencing information from Dr. Campbell's Reiki Master manual "Become a Reiki Master".

Usui Holy Fire Reiki Level III/ART & Reiki Master Class Outline (3 days)

Day One

- Logistics & Safety: Share start/end time of class, break policy, location of restrooms/exits/water. (5min)
- Review of materials needed for class: (5min)
    - Class manuals: "Learn to Practice Reiki", "Become a Reiki Master", and optionally "Teach Reiki Your Way" (have them write their name inside each)
    - Quartz Crystal in bag
    - Journal/something to write in & with
- Intros – Ask students to share their name, what energy healing training they have, and their expectations for the class (20-30min)
- Share your Reiki story with the students (5-10min)

Usui Holy Fire Reiki Level III/ART & Reiki Master Class Outline (cont.)

- Holy Love Guided Experience - Winding River, journaling & share (15-30min)
- Chapter 1: Setting a Foundation (30min)
- Chapter 2: Reiki Level III/Art (30min)
- Chapter 2: ... The Healing Power of Crystals Crystals (30min)
- Chapter 2: ... Exploring the Chakra System (30-60min)
- Chapter 2: ... Reiki Master Symbol (20min)

Lunch & Symbol Practice (60min)

- Dai Ko Myo Symbol "test"
- Holy Fire Usui Reiki Master Pre-Ignition
- Chapter 2: ... Understanding Attunements (30-60min)
- Attunement to Dai Ko Myo, journaling & share (30-60min)
- Demonstrate a Healing Attunement (10min)

Usui Holy Fire Reiki Level III/ART & Reiki Master Class Outline (cont.)

- Practice in groups 2-3 giving each other Healing Attunements and have each student create their own "Quick Guide"(45-60min)
- Closing meditation of your choice.

The chapters and meditations listed are referencing information from Dr. Campbell's Reiki class manuals "Learn to Practice Reiki", "Become a Reiki Master", and "Teach Reiki Your Way".

Usui Holy Fire Reiki Level III/ART & Reiki Master Class Outline (cont.)

Day Two

- Check-in with students - How is everyone feeling? Any questions come up overnight? (30-60min)
- Holy Love Experience - Winding River, journaling & share (15-30min)
- Chapter 3: ... Becoming a Reiki Master (10min)
- Chapter 3: ... Usui Holy Fire Reiki & Holy Fire Symbol (20min)
- Holy Fire Usui Reiki Master Ignition I, journaling & share (30-45min)
- Chapter 3: ... Reiki Level I, II, III/ART Attunements (15-30min) (Skip Usui Holy Fire Reiki Master Ignitions for now)

Lunch (60min)

- Practice in groups 2-3 giving each other Healing Attunements using Holy Fire and have each student create their own "Quick Guide" (60min)

Usui Holy Fire Reiki Level III/ART & Reiki Master Class Outline (cont.)

- Demonstrate a Reiki Level I Attunement (10min)
- Practice in groups 2-3 giving each other Reiki Level I Attunements and have each student create their own "Quick Guide" (60min)
- Closing meditation of your choice.

Note:

If you have extra time, feel free to move into Level II Attunements.

Usui Holy Fire Reiki Level III/ART & Reiki Master Class Outline (cont.)

Day Three

- Check-in with students - How is everyone feeling? Any questions come up overnight? (30-60min)
- Holy Fire Usui Reiki Master Ignition II, journaling & share (30-45min)
- Demonstrate a Reiki Level II Attunement and have each student create their own "Quick Guide" (10min)
- Practice in groups 2-3 giving each other Reiki Level II Attunements and have each student create their own "Quick Guide" (30-45min)
- Demonstrate a Reiki Level III Attunement (10min)
- Practice in groups 2-3 giving each other Reiki Level III Attunements and have each student create their own "Quick Guide" (30-45min)

Lunch (60min)

Usui Holy Fire Reiki Level III/ART & Reiki Master Class Outline (cont.)

- Chapter 3: ... Usui Holy Fire Reiki Master Ignitions (30min)
- Chapter 4: Teaching Reiki (Option to move into Dr. Campbell's teaching guide, "Teach Reiki Your Way" or stay in "Become a Reiki Master") (60-120min)
- Hand out Certificates
- Closing meditation of your choice.

<u>Note:</u>
Times listed are approximate and will vary based on number of students and the questions asked.

Holy Fire Reiki Master can be taught as a standalone 2-day course, however, you must somehow give the Holy Fire Reiki Master Pre-ignition to the students within 72 hours of the first Master Ignition. More information is available in "Become a Reiki Master".

The chapters and meditations listed are referencing information from Dr. Campbell's Reiki class manuals "Learn to Practice Reiki", "Become a Reiki Master", and "Teach Reiki Your Way".

Alternative & Online Reiki Class Outlines

Alternative Reiki Class Outlines

In addition to the more standard Reiki classes offered, the following outlines are great when you or your students need a little bit of flexibility.

Remember that the offerings in this book are merely guidelines and suggestions. Feel free to play with these outlines and come up with something that works best for you.

Community Healing Attunement

The Community Healing Attunement is a great way to give back and has been offered in multiple ways by various Reiki Masters around the world.

(Please note that if you were not trained specifically on how to do a Healing Attunement, it is NOT the same as a Reiki Attunement. If you are unsure, please reference Dr. Campbell's book "Become a Reiki Master" for information on how to do a Healing Attunement.)

The outline shared below is just the basics and can be added to just about any event being held. Get creative and see where you might be able to use it to share the power of Reiki with your community.

Room setup: Chairs should be in a circle, facing each other, with room for you to move around and between them)

Community Healing Attunement

- Welcome, personal introduction and any logistical information
- Option to do group introductions: ask students to share name and what brought them here.
- Share a bit about what Reiki is and how it works.
- Share about what a Healing Attunement is and ask them to take a few moments to think about a current issue or obstacle in their lives.
- Invite participants to close their eyes, lead a brief centering meditation to help them begin to focus inward.
- Begin the Healing Attunement
- Once complete, gently guide the group to come back into their bodies and open their eyes.
- Provide time for journaling and offer the opportunity for individuals to share if they would like.
- Perform closing of your choice.

Teaching Reiki across multiple Weeks

There are several reasons why you may choose to teach Reiki across multiple weeks.

For example, when teaching a student one-on-one, you can craft the outline to fit a schedule that works for you both. Typically it follows a 2-3 week layout, but you can work with your student to adjust as necessary.

If you are teaching one-on-one, be sure to raise your rate so you are being compensated appropriately. In a class with 6 students, 8hrs of class provides you with somewhere around $800-1200. If you are teaching one-on-one be sure you take that into consideration. For example, Dr. Campbell's Reiki I/II certification class costs $425/person, but a one-on-one Reiki Level I/II certification costs $825 for 8hrs across 4weeks, or more if the student wants more time.

The other common reason to teach across multiple weeks, is to provide a class more accessible to individual who don't have full 8hr days free for training. In this case you could offer a class once a week that was 2-3 hours long, and spread across 3-4 weeks.

The risk with this option is having students no-show (illness, work, etc.) and figuring out how to make-up that material with them, which can be tricky. A no-show also alters the container of the class energetically.

If you choose to go this route, be sure your refund and make-up policy is stated clearly in any communication or invoicing you do.

It is a kind offering for those who have tight schedules, however it can become difficult for you as the teacher. Remember that when it's right, it's right, and those who are meant for you will find you. If you feel called to offer class this way, great, but be careful not to let the pressure of scarcity "force" you into it.

Online Reiki Class Outlines

Dr. Campbell has successfully taught Reiki Level I & II as well as her other associated Reiki courses , such as Energy Healing for Mental Health multiple times online with great feedback from her students.

What makes her courses different than most is the extra time in-between Level I & II, as well as the addition of mentoring sessions, which provide the opportunity for specific help and feedback to be given to each student as they begin their practice.

With these alterations to a standard Reiki course, Dr, Campbell found that her students connected more deeply with Reiki and more easily implemented Reiki practices into their daily life.

The mentoring sessions should take place during the week after the online class, giving them time to practice before the call.

Online Reiki Class Outlines

It is important to note that Dr. Campbell's online courses also cost a bit more than her in-person offerings because of the additional hours of mentoring each student receives. As a teacher you will need to decide for yourself what price feels right for you.

Remember these outlines are merely guidelines, suggestions, for you to build from.

Online Class Prep Email

Greetings,

I'm excited to share the magic of Reiki with you! Below is some info to help you prepare for the class.

Note: I need you to email me back with the name you want on your certificate by (enter date here).

Class Date:
Time:

Class Link: https://zoom.us/j/85736332

A few bits of guidance...

- Please have a journal or notebook and something to write with (in addition to the materials I've mailed you).

- Dress comfortably, and feel free to wear fluffy socks or wrap up in a blanket.

Online Class Prep Email (cont.)

- You are also invited to use meditation cushions, or things of that nature to sit on/with. I like my students to be comfy in the way that works best for them so you don't need to be sitting at a desk or table. Take some time finding a comfy spot this week before class starts. We will be moving between meditation and conversation throughout the class.

- There are no planned breaks, but I usually try to take one every hour or so, or as needed.

- To physically prepare: do your best to abstain from, or minimize alcohol, meat products, caffeine, and maintain a "clean" diet. Not a requirement, just do what feels right for your body. And be sure to do your best to get a good night's sleep before class.

Online Class Prep Email (cont.)

- To mentally prepare: try to spend some time in meditation every day, play attention to your dreams, and any other synchronicities that might occur.

- You will be required to keep your camera on for the entire class, so please be sure that you are situated so that will be comfortable for you.

Technology requirements:

Laptop or desktop computer, or tablet with a camera and audio. Please do not attempt to attend this training on your phone.

Mentoring Sessions:

If you haven't scheduled your mentoring session yet, please reply to this email (or insert a scheduling link here).

Online Class Prep Email (Cont.)

If you have any other questions please let me know. My cell is (phone number here) in case you need to text/call me. I am looking forward to our class together.

See you Saturday!

(Your name here)

Note

If you are holding a Level II class include a copy of the Level II symbols in the email, explain that they will be learning about them in class and ask that they start practicing drawing them. (Full page Level II symbols for student copies are available in Dr. Campbell's book "Become a Reiki Master")

Usui Reiki Level I
Online Class Outline (6hrs)

- Logistics & Safety: Share start/end time of class, break policy, plan for dealing with tech issues. (5min)
- Review of materials needed for class: (5min)
    - Class manual: "Learn to Practice Reiki"
    - Journal/something to write in & with
- Intros – Ask students to share their name, any experience with energy healing, and their expectations for the class (20-30min)
- Share your Reiki story with the students (5-10min)
- Holy Love Guided Experience - Winding River, journaling & share (15-30min)
- Chapter 1: Getting to know the Energetic Body (60min)
- Chapter 2: Understanding Reiki Energy (60min)

Usui Reiki Level I
Online Class Outline (cont.)

- Chapter 3: Energy Healing Techniques (60min)
- Level 1 attunement, journaling, & share (30-60min)
- Practice flowing Reiki as a group with hands in prayer (Gassho) position (10-15min)
- Guide students through practice of a self-healing using standard hand placements, journaling, group share (30-45min)
- Closing meditation of your choice.

**email out certificates after class ends

<u>Notes</u>:

Times listed are approximate and will vary based on number of students and the questions asked. When you take lunch will vary on your start/end time but is suggested before or after Chapter 3 if possible.

The chapters and meditations listed are referencing information from Dr. Campbell's Reiki class manuals "Learn to Practice Reiki" and "Become a Reiki Master".

Usui Reiki Level II
Online Class Outline (6hrs)

- Logistics & Safety: Share start/end time of class, break policy, plan for dealing with tech issues. (5min)
- Review of materials needed for class: (5min)
    - Class manual: "Learn to Practice Reiki"
    - Quartz Crystal in bag
    - Journal/something to write in & with
- Intros – Ask students to share their name, any experience with energy healing, and their expectations for the class (20-30min)
- Share your Reiki story with the students (5-10min)
- Holy Love Guided Experience - Waterfall, journaling & share (15-30min)
- Chapter 4: The Healing Power of Crystals (30-60min)

Usui Reiki Level II
Online Class Outline (cont.)

- Chapter 5: Using Reiki Energy with Others (30min)
- Chapter 6: Usui Holy Fire Reiki Level II Symbols (60min)

Lunch & Symbol Practice (30min)

- Level II Symbol "Test" (30min)
- Level II attunement, journaling, & share (30-60min)
- Guide students through a distance Reiki session (20min)
- Guide students through using Choku Rei to seal and clear the space. (15min)
- Chapter 7: Working with Reiki in Everyday life (60min)
- Chapter 8: Doing Business as a Reiki Practitioner (optional)

Usui Reiki Level II
Online Class Outline (cont.)

- Explain that over the next week they should work with a friend, family member, or "teddy bear" stand-in to practice giving session to others.
- Closing meditation of your choice

**email out certificates after class ends

Notes:

Times listed are approximate and will vary based on number of students and the questions asked. When you take lunch will vary on your start/end time, but should occur before the attunement.

The chapters and meditations listed are referencing information from Dr. Campbell's Reiki class manuals "Learn to Practice Reiki" and "Become a Reiki Master".

Usui Reiki Level I/II Online Class Outline
(2 Days with one week in between)

Day one:

- Logistics & Safety: Share start/end time of class, break policy, plan for dealing with tech issues. (5min)
- Review of materials needed for class: (5min)
    - Class manual: "Learn to Practice Reiki"
    - Quartz Crystal in bag
    - Journal/something to write in & with
- Intros – Ask students to share their name, any experience with energy healing, and their expectations for the class (20-30min)
- Share your Reiki story with the students (5-10min)
- Holy Love Guided Experience - Winding River, journaling & share (15-30min)

Usui Reiki Level I/II Online Class Outline (cont.)

- Chapter 1: Getting to know the Energetic Body (60min)
- Chapter 2: Understanding Reiki Energy (60min)
- Chapter 3: Energy Healing Techniques (60min)
- Level 1 attunement, journaling, & share (30-60min)
- Practice flowing Reiki as a group with hands in prayer (Gassho) position (10-15min)
- Guide students through practice of a self-healing using standard hand placements, journaling, group share (30-45min)
- Provide students with a copy of the level II symbols, briefly explaining each one and that they will need to verbally name and draw each one by memory the following day.
- Closing meditation of your choice.

Usui Reiki Level I/II Online Class Outline (cont.)

Notes:

Times listed are approximate and will vary based on number of students and the questions asked. When you take lunch will vary on your start/end time but is suggested before or after Chapter 3 if possible.

In-between the Level I & II classes the teacher and student should have their mentoring call to address and specific questions or issues the students has.

The chapters and meditations listed are referencing information from Dr. Campbell's Reiki class manuals "Learn to Practice Reiki" and "Become a Reiki Master".

Usui Reiki Level I/II Online Class Outline (cont.)

Day Two (One week later)

- Check-in with students - How is everyone feeling? Any questions come up since last week?
- Holy Love Guided Experience - Waterfall, journaling & share (15-30min)
- Chapter 4: The Healing Power of Crystals (30-60min)
- Chapter 5: Using Reiki Energy with Others (30min)
- Chapter 6: Usui Holy Fire Reiki Level II Symbols (60min)

Lunch & Symbol Practice (30min)

- Level II Symbol "Test" (30min)
- Level II attunement, journaling, & share (30-60min)
- Guide students through a distance Reiki session (20min)

Usui Reiki Level I/II Online Class Outline (cont.)

- Guide students through using Choku Rei to seal and clear the space. (15min)
- Chapter 7: Working with Reiki in Everyday life (60min)
- Chapter 8: Doing Business as a Reiki Practitioner (optional)
- Explain that over the next week they should work with a friend, family member, or "teddy bear" stand-in to practice giving session to others.
- Closing meditation of your choice

**email out certificates after class ends

<u>Notes</u>:
Times listed are approximate and will vary based on number of students and the questions asked. When you take lunch will vary on your start/end time, but should occur before the attunement.

The chapters and meditations listed are referencing information from Dr. Campbell's Reiki class manuals "Learn to Practice Reiki" and "Become a Reiki Master".

Guided Meditations & Experiences

Body Scan Meditation

Begin by taking a few deep breaths to allow your mind to clear. Just breathe slowly and calmly, taking your time with each breath.

Breathe at your own pace...allowing each breath to come as it may, without any conscious effort to change your breathing.

This will be an exercise of observing. You will do a body scan and observe each part of your body passively...just noticing, without the need to make any changes or to cause anything to occur.

You can simply watch and take note of any changes that happen on their own without any effort on your part. Let's begin the body scan.

Turn your attention to your toes. Focus on your toes, just noticing how your toes feel right now. Notice each toe.

Body Scan Meditation (cont.)

Concentrate now on your right foot...just noticing your right foot without trying to change anything at all.

Now move your attention to your left foot...noticing how your left foot feels.

Observe both feet. How do your feet feel? Notice the temperature of your feet. Can you feel anything touching your feet? Clothing, the floor, the air? Notice how your feet feel inside. Heavy? Light? Loose? Tight? Make these passive observations...you are simply an observer...not providing any input at all.

Continue the body scan up to your ankles. Passively notice your ankles. Feel your ankles. Breathe.

Moving up now to your lower legs. Focus on your lower legs. Concentrate all of your attention simply on observing how your lower legs feel right now.

Body Scan Meditation (cont.)

Noticing. Observing. Completely passive...not trying to change anything.

Mentally scan your knees. Notice and observe each knee. Then take note of how your upper legs are feeling.

Notice your legs...taking note of any passive observations you become aware of. Just noticing...and then letting your attention move to the next area of the body.

Now notice your hips...

Your lower abdomen...

Moving up now all the way to the center of your body, at the level of your belly button...scanning your body...just noticing how the core of your body feels. Mentally watch and observe...taking in the details of how your body is feeling.

Body Scan Meditation (cont.)

Do a passive scan without making any changes or trying to make anything happen.

Now notice your middle back. Observe how your back feels.

Scan your sides...chest...and upper back.

Noticing. Observing.

Turn your attention now to your fingertips. How do the tips of your fingers feel?

Continue...thoroughly scanning your body to observe how each area is feeling. Take note of your hands...notice the palms of your hands, and the backs of your hands. Breathe.

Scan your wrists...lower arms...elbows....

Body Scan Meditation (cont.)

Turn your attention to your upper arms...noticing...observing...taking in your observations of how your upper arms are feeling.

Notice your shoulders. Scanning the front...sides...back...and top of your shoulders.

Scan your arms as a whole...noticing passively...allowing...watching...completely free of effort or direction from you.

Continue all the way up to your neck. Notice and observe your neck...the front of your neck...each side...the back of your neck.

Moving your attention up now to your chin...lips...cheeks...

Observe your nose...eyes...forehead...the top of your head...your ears....

Body Scan Meditation (cont.)

Keeping this attitude of passive observation, mentally scan your body now as a whole. Do a complete scan, at your own pace, from your feet to your head.

If you notice anything of interest, you may choose to allow your attention to linger there for a moment as you observe how your muscles and tissues are feeling.

Go ahead now and do a complete body scan, mentally observing your entire body.

You are fully aware now of how your body is feeling, and you have completed a body scan.
Notice how you are feeling now, mentally and physically, overall.

Observe any changes that may have occurred, all on their own.

And when you are ready, only when you are ready, there is no rush... I invite you to open your eyes.

Protective Light Meditation

I invite you to get comfortable, finding a position that will allow your body to begin to relax.

Take a deep breath in, and as you exhale, let the tension start to leave your body. Take slow, calm breaths.

Mentally scan your body, taking note of how your body feels. Focus in on the areas where tension is stored and concentrate on relaxing those areas.

Feel your body becoming more relaxed... slowly releasing tension... letting go of stress...

Noticing that you are relaxing more and more...

Imagine that there is a protective light shining around your body... almost as if you are glowing. This light can keep you safe right now from stress, tension, worries, and other problems that have seemed to bother you.

Protective Light Meditation (cont.)

Picture in your mind being surrounded by light. Feel how relaxed, calm, and secure you feel as this protective light surrounds you. The light is like a shield, deflecting anything that is not good. It is like a spiritual armor that can protect you and help you to feel calm and relaxed.

Imagine being surrounded by this protective light…. from your head to your feet…..

Focus your attention on your feet…. feeling how relaxed and maybe even tingly your feet feel. Notice that your feet are surrounded by protective light….. as are your ankles…. let your ankles be loose and relaxed.

Feel your lower legs relaxing, surrounded by light….. soft…. heavy….. relaxed. Your upper legs are relaxed and surrounded by light too….. very warm and relaxed.

Protective Light Meditation (cont.)

Turn your attention now to your hands..... feel the relaxation there as your hands become very relaxed.... limp..... heavy...... along with your wrists, lower arms.... and upper arms.... all surrounded and protected, shielded by protective light.

Feel the relaxation in the core of your body... starting at your stomach... and flowing outward.... feel the relaxation flowing from the center of your body, out to your back.... chest..... hips..... feel the relaxation filling your body. Notice that your body is enclosed in a shield of light as well.

Allow the relaxation to continue to flow through your body, upward to your neck and shoulders.... all the way to the top of your head. Feel your face relaxing.... limp and relaxed.... calm .... and feel the protective light surrounding your head and face, your whole body....

Protective Light Meditation (cont.)

You are surrounded from head to toe in protective light.... shielded from any worries or troubles.
Relax.... basking in protective light.

(pause)

Notice that there might still be some areas of tension in your body.... some worries remaining in your mind. You might even be able to picture these areas of tension as dark. See the dark tension being drawn out of your body by the protective light. Feel the worries and stress leaving your body and mind as they are leaving your body.

The protective light is like a magnet, drawing out the dark tension, out of your body and away... once the tension has left your body it is repelled by the light, which works as a shield, protecting you from anything that is not in your best interest.

Protective Light Meditation (cont.)

The light also works as a magnet for good, peaceful thoughts…. attracting relaxation to you.

Feel the protective light drawing away tension, and bringing forth relaxation….. shielding and protecting you, while helping you to feel even more relaxed.

Enjoy this feeling of being safe and protected by your spiritual shield of protective light.

(pause)

You are so calm….. so relaxed…. peaceful…. relaxed.

(pause)

Now it is time to return to your day. Remember that you can imagine this protective light again, any time you need to, and can repel stress and tension and feel calm and relaxed.

Protective Light Meditation (cont.)

Focus again on your breathing.... taking a deep breath in..... and out....

Now turn your attention to your body reawakening. Gently move your body a little, feeling your muscles waking up.

Stretch a bit if you like.
Allow your mind to become fully awake and alert, while still feeling relaxed.

When you are ready, open your eyes.... fully awake, energized and calm.

Holy Love Experience – Winding River

You find yourself in the middle of a beautiful valley. In front of you there is a forest and all around you there are beautiful mountains reaching high up into the sky. The weather is just perfect, not too hot, not too cold, and you can feel a slight breeze playing upon your skin as the sun warms you. As you look around you, you notice a path laid out before you that leads towards the forest. You begin to follow this path and as you enter the forest you notice the light begins to dim a bit from the tree coverage, and the air gets a bit cooler, and maybe even a bit damp.

Though you can't explain it, you know you are safe here. That you are being watched over and protected.

You continue down the path and begin to hear the sound of rushing water. As you come around a bend in the path you notice a river off to the right.

Holy Love Experience – Winding River (cont.)

You begin to walk down towards the river, and once you get to the river's edge you notice a bright beam of sunlight shining down from the sky, reflecting gently across the water. As you look into the light, you realize this is no normal beam of light, but rather a light that is shining down from the highest of heavens, just for you. Take a few moments here to allow yourself to receive whatever guidance this light has for you.

(Stop talking and allow the students to stay in this space for about 10-15 min. When it is time to return, guide the students back.

I invite you to begin to feel yourself coming fully back into your body, back into this room. When you are ready, and only when you are ready, I invite you to take a few deep breaths, maybe wiggle your fingers, your toes. And once you feel fully present, I invite you to gently open your eyes. Please take a few moments to reflect on your experience in your journals.

Holy Love Experience – Waterfall

You find yourself in the middle of a beautiful valley. In front of you there is a forest and all around you there are beautiful mountains reaching high up into the sky. The weather is just perfect, not too hot, not too cold, and you can feel a slight breeze playing upon your skin as the sun warms you. As you look around you, you notice a path laid out before you that leads towards the forest. You begin to follow this path and as you enter the forest you notice the light begins to dim a bit from the tree coverage, and the air gets a bit cooler, and maybe even a bit damp.

Though you can't explain it, you know you are safe here. That you are being watched over and protected.

You continue down the path and begin to hear the sound of rushing water. As you come around a bend in the path you notice a river off to the right, but decide to keep walking.

Holy Love Experience – Waterfall (cont.)

The further you walk, the louder the sound of the water gets, and you begin to see the path opening up in the distance to what looks like a waterfall.

As you get closer you see the most beautiful waterfall cascading down into a large pool of crystal clear water. At this point you may decide to wade into the water, or you may choose to sit on a rock near the water's edge.

As you begin to relax, enjoying the mist of the waterfall, you notice a bright beam of light coming down from the heavens. The light plays across the water, and eventually finds it's way to you. The light shines on you, through you, surrounds you. Be one with this light and allow it to guide you.

Stop talking and allow the students to stay in this space for about 10-15 minutes.

Holy Love Experience – Waterfall (cont.)

When it is time to return, guide the students back.

I invite you to begin to feel yourself coming fully back into your body, back into this room. When you are ready, and only when you are ready, I invite you to take a few deep breaths, maybe wiggle your fingers, your toes. And once you feel fully present, I invite you to gently open your eyes. Please take a few moments to reflect on your experience in your journals.

© 2025, Adrian Campbell, PhD

.

www.ingramcontent.com/pod-product-compliance
Lightning Source LLC
Chambersburg PA
CBHW072143160426
43197CB00012B/2226